PERFORMING TRIBUTE 9/11: ORDINARY PEOPLE, REMARKABLE STORIES

DONNA KAZ

ISBN: 978-1-950201-01-3

ISBN: 978-1-950201-02-0

Cover Photo by Deb Di Grigorio

❀ Created with Vellum

For all we lost and all we found.

Cast

- **Desiree Bouchat** – survivor, south tower

- **Bridget Damiano** – recovery volunteer, family member

- **Gail Langsner** – area resident survivor

- **Kate Richardson** – FDNY family member

- **Ann Van Hine** – FDNY family member

- **Gerry Bogacz** – survivor, north tower

- **Ray Habib** – family member

- **Paul McFadden** – FDNY retired, recovery worker

- **Bob Nussburger** – first responder, volunteer FDNY

- ***Anthony Palmeri*** – recovery worker, NY Dept. of Sanitation

Setting

10 chairs and 10 music stands. The play is to be read from scripts. Simple staging may be added near the beginning and the end of the play.

Performing Tribute is a theatrical telling of the stories of Desiree Bouchet, Bridget Damiano, Gail Langsner, Kate Richardson, Ann Van Hine, Gerry Bogacz, Ray Habib, Paul McFadden, Bob Nussburger and Anthony Palmeri.

We have learned that loss and suffering are not healed by silence and ignorance and that everyone has a story. We hope that as you work on presenting Performing Tribute you will be inspired to tell yours.
    -Donna Kaz

PART I: INTRO

SOUND - MUSIC INTRO. LIGHTS UP: Lights rise on cast sitting in front of music stands. IF POSSIBLE the title, *"PERFORMING TRIBUTE 9/11: Ordinary People, Remarkable Stories,"* is projected onto the back wall.

GERRY

Welcome to a presentation of Performing Tribute 9/11: Ordinary People, Remarkable Stories. You will hear from survivors, family members, first responders, volunteer workers and New York City residents whose lives were forever changed on September 11, 2001. My name is Gerry. I worked at the World Trade Center on the 82nd floor of the North Tower.

ANN

I'm Ann. My husband, Bruce, was a New York City Fire-fighter with Squad 41.

BRIDGET

My name is Bridget and I lost my cousin, Joe, in the South Tower. I was also a volunteer with the Salvation Army during the rescue and recovery efforts.

BOB

I'm Bob and I always wanted to be a New York City Firefighter. On Sept 11th my wife woke me up and said "Bob, a plane just crashed into the World Trade Center". I got up and watched it on TV just like everybody else…but only I knew that I was going there.

GAIL

I'm Gail. I live right across the street from where the South Tower stood.

DESIREE

My name is Desiree and I worked in the South Tower on the 101st floor. Most offices opened at 9am but my office opened at 8:30 and, being the good employee that I am, on September 11th I was at my desk at 8am.

RAY

My name is Ray and my wife, Barbara, worked for an insurance company that had offices on a number of floors in the north tower.

KATE

I'm Kate and I was born in 1972 and grew up in New Jersey so as far as I was concerned the twin towers always existed. I worked in midtown Manhattan and when I would come up out of the subway all I had to do was to look for where the towers were to orient myself. My husband of three years, Bob, was a NYC firefighter and he had gone into work on September 10th for a 24 hour shift.

ANTHONY

My name is Anthony and I worked for the New York City Department of Sanitation for 23 years. After September 11th, I volunteered to work at the site.

PAUL

Hi, I'm Paul. I'm retired from the New York City Fire Department. A third of all the people in the world watched or listened to what happened on 9/11 on the TV or radio. Together our stories paint a picture of both horrible tragedy and tremendous humanity. September 11, 2001 is the day that 2,977 people were murdered on US soil due to a hostile attack. 2,753 of those were in New York City at the World Trade Center.

LIGHTS / SOUND - a short pause.

PART II: SEPTEMBER 11TH

GERRY

When the twin towers were opened in 1973 they were the tallest and second tallest buildings in the world. Each tower had 110 stories and stood just 131 feet apart. Unlike the classic skyscrapers of the day they did not taper as they rose, they were the same dimensions from the ground all the way to the roofline. There were a total of 7 buildings in the World Trade Center complex. Every day 50 thousand people worked there, 100 thousand visited and tens of thousands came through the underground transportation terminal, up through the huge shopping mall and into lower Manhattan.

RAY

My wife and I had never been to the observation deck at top of the South Tower. Being New Yorkers we never did touristy things. But the weekend before 9/11 the weather was great and we decided to go up. I'll never forget how beautiful the view was from the top of the towers.

ANTHONY

Everyone knows exactly where they were on September 11, 2001. It was a Tuesday and in New York City it was an absolutely gorgeous, gorgeous, day. The sky was crystal clear blue. Pilots have a term for weather like that. They call it severe clear.

BRIDGET

September 11th was a unique day in New York because it was a primary election day and the first day of school for young children. The night before the New York Giants played the Denver Broncos in a Monday Night football game that lasted well past midnight. And all of those little things all turned out to be good because people were getting to work late. Instead of 50 thousand people at the World Trade Center on 9/11, it was only 30% full which is about 17,500 people.

DESIREE

At 7:59am American Airlines flight #11 leaves Boston's Logan airport for Los Angeles. Terrorists hijack the plane. It is estimated that they use the Hudson River as a guide and fly the plane south at an increasingly low altitude.

KATE

At 8:46AM the plane crashes into the north face of the North Tower at almost 500 miles per hour. It hits the tower very high up, between the 92 and 98th floors. Immediately upon impact a jet fuel fireball erupts and shoots down the center core of the building causing explosions in the lobby and concourse level.

PAUL

Everyone on the 92nd floor and above who survives the initial impact is trapped.

GERRY

Because the towers were so tall, they had to withstand enormous wind loads and were constructed to sway about three and a half feet at the roofline. Now when the first plane struck the north face of the North Tower that was not enough to knock the tower over because the wind load on any one of the building's faces was much more than that. But the three and a half feet sway happened in an instant. I heard an explosion above me and the building immediately jumped three and a half feet to the south and then stood back up again. In my office on the 82nd floor debris came down from the ceiling and some people were knocked off their feet. I knew it wasn't a good thing. When something like that happens you just go. Because so many people were trapped above us we got down the stairs fairly quickly. We were led out of the stairwell at the 43rd floor to change to a different stairwell. There was a big movement of people in lobby. For me this was the worse part of the evacuation. I remember looking out the window and seeing a whole bunch of paper in the air and thinking that something was still happening. One of the elevator doors was slightly open and there was black smoke coming out. I felt really trapped and was trying to figure out what to do. Should I stay in the line I am in or go back to the stairwell I came from? I decided to go back. I continued to walk down the stairs with a lot of other people and came out on the underground concourse level.

GAIL

My polling place was a High School south of Liberty Street and I was voting when the first plane hit. I felt the concussion and then the lights in the lobby flickered and went out and then came back on again. All the kids started to cheer because they thought some electrical transformer had blown up and they were going to get a day off school. We went outside and there were papers flying hundreds of feet up. It looked a tornado but there was no wind. People were starting to stream away saying something blew up in the Trade Center. My aunt in California called and said they're saying a plane hit the North Tower but that's the one away from you guys right? So you're OK, right? And for 17 minutes we were OK.

RAY

The people on the north side of the South Tower were looking over at the North Tower. They could see the smoke and fire; they could feel the heat; and they could see people falling from the building. People who were facing south in the South Tower couldn't see what was happening and had a different reaction.

ANTHONY

Announcements were made in the South Tower that the building was secure and that people should not evacuate, they should go back to their offices. This was standard procedure, given the problem was in the other tower.

BOB

Of course, no one knew a second plane was coming.

DESIREE

My desk was on the south side of the South Tower. When the plane hit the North Tower this is what I heard, (boom), nothing louder, just (boom). The lights flickered and my computer went off and then back on. People started to joke that we forgot to pay the utility bill again. A friend of mine at 7 WTC called to ask me if I was okay. I said, "yes, why?" She said she had heard a bomb had gone off somewhere. My office Manager, Jim, walked past and said that his wife had just called him and told him that a plane had gone into Tower 1. That made sense to me. When you are on the 101st floor of a building, planes and helicopters fly below you. That a putt-putt plane didn't quite make it to Newark Airport actually made sense. Jim said "I think we should leave." It wasn't even 9:00am.

ANN

I had stopped by my dance studio to check messages and got back in the car and now I know that it was about 5 after 9 and I turned the radio on and heard that a plane had hit one of the trade towers. I personally thought what kind of ding-a-ling would do that because it was a beautiful day and they were saying it was a small plane. And then as I put the car into reverse they announced that another plane hit. And as I got on the highway to head home there was an announcement over the radio for all firefighters to report for duty. My husband, Bruce, was already on duty but I knew that the fire department does not issue total recalls and that they had never done something like that. I just thought – OK, we're at war.

GERRY

Because people were voting or taking their children to school there were only about 17 thousand people in the towers as opposed to 50 thousand in the entire complex. The timing of the attacks was bad for firefighters though because their shifts rotated at 9am. Firefighters who were getting off duty stayed on to respond. They were joined by firefighters just reporting to work. Some firehouses had double the number of firefighters than they normally had responding to the Trade Center.

RAY

There are so many stories that you will hear of people who were supposed to be at the World Trade Center but were not. My wife's story is just the opposite. She was not supposed to be there. She worked for one of the largest insurance companies in the world but her office was midtown Manhattan. As fate would have it her company had a number of floors in the North Tower and she had a meeting on the 99th floor of the North Tower on September 11th. The meeting was at 9AM but "Miss Punctual" that she was she arrived at 8:30. So when I heard that the first plane hit the first thing I did was to call her on her cell phone. It went into voice mail and I was very happy to hear her voice. Then, later on, I kept trying to phone her and there was absolutely nothing. So knowing that she was on the 99th floor, in looking back, I realized that she was right where the first plane hit.

KATE

I was working up in midtown right across the street from Radio City Music Hall. My college roommate called me right after the first plane hit and said a plane just flew into the World Trade Center. My husband of three years, Bob, was a NYC firefighter and he had gone into work the night before for a 24-hour shift. He had only been on the job two years and at that time he was working at Engine 23 in Manhattan. I called the firehouse right away but the line was busy and I thought he's far enough away from those buildings downtown so he's not going to be the first one to respond.

PAUL

17 minutes after the first plane left Boston's Logan airport another plane, United flight 175, also takes off from Boston heading for Los Angeles. It is hijacked and changes direction towards New York.

DESIREE

At a little before 9am I got on a local elevator with 2 of my colleagues and saw that Jim was walking down the hall making sure that everyone had left. We got to the 78th floor sky-lobby and got out. The lobby was packed with about 400 people all waiting for the elevators and trying to make calls on their cell phones. It was calm but there was a lot of nervous joking and talking so it was very noisy but there was no panic. An express elevator door opened right next to me and I got on and went down with 4 of my coworkers and 51 strangers. When we reached the lobby the police and fire department instructed us to leave via the concourse level one flight below. I could see broken glass and fires on Liberty Street and UPS and FedEx mail envelopes strewn everywhere. We walked through the mall and up onto the street. I had only gone about 10 steps when I heard one of my co-workers yelled "Run!"

BRIDGET

My cousin Joe and I grew up in a close knit Italian family in New Jersey. After working his way through college Joe landed his dream job as a financial analyst. Joe's office was in the South Tower facing north. He saw the first plane hit the North Tower and called his wife and left a voice message that said: "Marie, its Joe. A plane just hit World Trade Center One. I'm OK, I'm on the 94th floor. I can feel the heat from the explosion and I just saw some guy jump out. You can't call me. I'll call you when I can. Just so you know." Through his colleagues we know that he did evacuate to the 78th floor sky lobby but when they made the announcement for everyone to go back to their offices he got back on an elevator. The stamp on his wife's message machine read 9:02am.

ANTHONY

Flight 175 is flying over New Jersey when it makes a sharp turn around the Statue of Liberty and at 9:03am slams into the southeast side of the South Tower entering between the 78th and 84th floors. When it comes in it tips a little bit and because it tips one stairwell is left intact all the way to the top. About 18 people are lucky enough to find that stairwell and evacuate but 500 or so are above the impact zone and remain trapped in the South tower.

BOB

I got dressed real quick I ran around to my fire house a few blocks away. There was a couple of guys there already and they said the teletype was going crazy so I said let's get some extra equipment and put it on the ambulance so we'll be ready. I was the captain, I had one guy that was a medic, one guy was an EMT and one guy was a driver and radioman. The telephone rang and it was emergency medical services and they wanted to know if we had any units available. I said yes, we got one unit available and could have another two ready in 20 minutes. They said OK you are going to the World Trade Center. So we took off and 14 minutes later we were there.

PAUL

American Airlines Flight 77 from Washington Dulles Airport to Los Angeles slams into the western side of the Pentagon at 9:37am. The section it hits consists of renovated offices that are mostly unoccupied. 125 people on the ground and all 59 passengers and crew on the plane are killed.

GERRY

When I came out of stairwell B and onto the concourse level there was water coming down from above and there was debris all over the floor. We were rushed out onto the street and people were yelling "Don't look back, keep moving!" which made a lot of sense because there was so many people behind us. I walked about half a block and then I did look back and was astounded to see both towers on fire, although I don't remember seeing smoke just the flames. I was thinking that part of the plane must have bounced off and hit Tower 2. And then I just needed to get to a phone to let my family know that I wasn't dead. I was really scared that my daughter, who was 9 years old at the time, was seeing this same image on television and did not know how I was.

BOB

We came up out of the Brooklyn Battery tunnel and pulled up near the South Tower. A police officer pointed to where we should park and said to hurry up because we were the next guys going in. So we moved the unit and got ready. An EMS captain told us to go into the South Tower and help some people who were burnt and trapped in an elevator. We started walking across the street but got stopped because there was debris coming down off the building. We got the go ahead to continue and just as we started we heard a rumble and looked up and here comes the building. By the time we heard the building coming down it was already half way down. The amount of pressure blowing out the bottom of the building lifted me up and took me from one side of the street to the other and the only thing that stopped me from going further was there was a lot of stuff falling on top of me pushing me into the ground.

ANN

The jet fuel from the planes caused fires in both towers that burned at 1800 to 2000 degrees. Steel looses 50% of its structural integrity at 2000 degrees and so the Tower's steel was starting to soften. You had the jet fuel that set all the paper on fire and all the office furniture and you had many floors that were fully engaged and so you had a tremendous amount of heat being generated. In the south tower, when the pinstriped steel that covered the building started to bow inward, the top of the tower tilted over and then the entire building collapsed. It took about 10 seconds for the South Tower to pancake down. It fell at 120 miles per hour.

KATE

I had an important meeting to go to at 10am. I got to the meeting room a little before 10 and there was a sign on the door that said the meeting had been canceled. So I got back in the elevator and when I got off at my floor people were screaming "the South Tower's collapsed".

GAIL

When the second plane came in and hit we ran to the windows in time to see the fireball and a lot of debris falling off the building. We thought we're on the top floor and something is going to come through the roof. We'll be safer if we go lower down in the building. I make my living as a pet sitter and I only take care of birds so my partner, Nat, and I packed up the 8 birds and went down to our friend's apartment on the third floor. We were sitting around their kitchen table trying to figure out what to do when my neighbor looked out the window and saw the top of the South Tower start to tilt and screamed to get in the back room. We ran into their back room, which has no windows and basically just prepared to die. There was a roar of noise, no individual sounds like glass breaking or metal tearing just a roar of noise. The building shook from things hitting it, the ground shook from the force of the collapse but definitely the most surreal thing was the pressure waves that happened as the building pancaked down which made it feel like my head was being squeezed in and out, in and out. Thank goodness Nat was there because that whole day, starting from the time my aunt called me, on the very surface of my brain I was thinking "someone is flying planes into office buildings" and then it would be like "Wait! Wait! What?" I could not process it.

PAUL

Tower Two was hit lower and so it had to hold up more weight that's why it collapsed first. When the South Tower came down it sliced the Marriott Hotel in half and trapped rescue workers and people inside. When the air from the collapse began to clear, firefighters went into the Marriott to rescue those who were trapped.

BRIDGET

Because of a congested runway United Flight 93 is delayed 40 minutes but takes off from Newark International Airport and heads for San Francisco. It flies close to the World Trade Center before heading west. It is hijacked, reverses direction over Ohio and begins to head east. The passengers on that flight learn about the World Trade Center attacks through cell and air phone calls and make a plan to storm the cockpit. The plane crashes in Shanksville, Pennsylvania at 10:03am.

RAY

Almost 30 minutes after the South Tower collapses the North Tower also falls in the same way, taking about 10 seconds to come down. Firefighters working to evacuate the North Tower have no idea that the South Tower has already collapsed and many are killed. The exact time of the North Tower collapse is 10:28. When the North Tower goes the entire Marriott Hotel is also destroyed.

ANTHONY

Imagine walking through a cloud or a snowstorm. That is what it was like for you if you lived near the Twin Towers. When the World Trace Center collapsed, everything came crashing through your apartment window and settled on your photos and your prized possessions. I worked for the NYC department of sanitation and I was not assigned to come down here, I volunteered to help with the clean up.

ANN

I went home after hearing the total recall on the radio and

then I watched both towers collapse on TV. I went to pick my two daughters up from school around 11am. As I was driving to pick them up from school I could see the New York City skyline and I saw the huge cloud of smoke. When I picked the girls their first question was "Where's Daddy?" and I said I don't know, we're going to wait until Daddy would be off duty to call the firehouse so we were going to wait to 8 o'clock. I made it to 7:30.

DESIREE

I decided to walk to Rockefeller Center because I had a friend who worked there. As I walked I saw people gathered around car radios listening to news reports about hijacked planes but I didn't really stop to listen. It took me several hours to walk to where my friend worked and when subway service was restored in the afternoon we took the subway to her house in Queens because I knew I couldn't get back to New Jersey. When we reached her apartment we turned the TV on and that was the first time I saw the plane go into Tower 2 and watched it come down. It wasn't until that moment that I realized that my office was gone.

GAIL

I was wearing flip flops and Nat said "Honey, you're going to have to put on shoes, we're going to have to run". He's also the one who knew that we had to take the birds with us because they wouldn't let us come back after we left. And I looked at him and said "Who's not going to let us come back? We live here!" We made one attempt to leave after the south tower came down and we couldn't see through the smoke and the dust. I have to tell you I was panicked, I would have run but Nat kept saying "Stop! We are going to get in more trouble climbing over flaming debris then if we just go back into the building." At 10:28 when the North Tower came down we had no clue what was happening. That whole day I never believed the two towers had collapsed. When we finally left it was about 11:30 in the morning. Nat figured out how to bundle up the bird carriers and hang them from a broomstick, which he carried across his shoulders. We looked like every picture of fleeing refugees you've ever seen.

ANTHONY

I was at work in Manhattan and my only thought was that I needed to get back home to New Jersey. It was so hard getting out of the City. I got in my car and tried to cross the George Washington Bridge but police were not letting anyone cross so I sat in traffic for a long time. People came up to my car and begged me to give them a ride into New Jersey. I was afraid to let anyone in but I finally let four people get in my car and the police waved us through. That's when I began to feel safe.

KATE

I commuted that day into the city from New Jersey. My husband and I were actually in the process of buying a new home and we'd just moved out of our old house the weekend before and were living at my parent's house for a few weeks. I took the bus into work that morning and for some reason I decided to sit in the front row of the bus, which I never do. I felt like a little old lady with my bagel and coffee sitting in the front row. We headed south on Route 17 and at one point on that route you get a beautiful view of the New York City skyline which I distinctly remember seeing that morning since I was in the front row of the bus. I remember being very happy and thinking "Wow, what a great skyline, what a beautiful day". That was the last time I would see that view.

BOB

Since 8:46, the time of the impact of American Airlines Flight 11 into the North Tower until its collapse, 102 minutes have passed.

LIGHTS / SOUND - a short pause.

PART III: AFTERMATH

BOB

I said to myself. "I'm dead." But then I started feeling a lot of pain. There wasn't too much rubble on top of me so I started to crawl out. I'm covered in blood and so I go the only way I can which is towards the Hudson River. I'm falling down and I'm getting back up and I can feel the adrenalin running through me and I'm thinking, "I know I'm gonna have a heart attack." When I get down by the water there's a New York City fireboat there and they take me along with a lot of other people over to New Jersey.

GAIL

We walk south and end up in a building that faces Battery Park that still has all their windows intact so we can get out of that air. I am wearing a white shirt and I keep trying to brush dirt off of it and then I realize that it isn't dirt, it's tiny burn holes. There was enough molten material flying around in the air to land on our clothes and burn through. I start to laugh that I am trying to brush burn holes off my shirt and I heard my voice start to go hysterical. I thought I can't lose it right now, there's just too much going on. And I didn't look anyone in the eye for the rest of the day.

PAUL

I was playing golf with a bunch of retired firemen and a guy came up to us and told us that planes hit the World Trade Center and both towers had collapsed. So we all changed clothes and jumped in my car and started for New York City. After going through check point after check point showing badges and ID's we finally get to the Midtown Tunnel where they have bomb-sniffing dogs go around the car. We finally get through and we drive as far as we can and then park and make our way down to the site. All the way in I'm saying to my friends when we get there we'll go right to the command post and right to Ray Downey. Ray Downey was the FDNY Chief of Special Operations and was probably the world's foremost expert on urban collapses. He was sent to Oklahoma City to help coordinate the search and rescue of the Federal Building out there and he's written many books on the subject. It is ironic that the first two people I see are his two sons, Chuck and Joe, who are both firemen. I go right up to them and I say "Joe, where's your Dad, where's the command post?" And he looks at me and says "Paul, we have to go home to our mother because our father is under this rubble".

ANN

I stop by to touch base with my parents and my Dad keeps saying to my girls there's no way your Dad is there because his firehouse is a long way from the Trade Center. My Dad is thinking that Bruce would have been sent out after the second plane hit but he was not tuning into the fact that Bruce was in Squad 41. A squad is special operations unit so even with regular fires Squad 41 comes into Manhattan. So I know even as my Dad is saying Bruce can't be there because of the time I know he is there because he is in a squad. But I wasn't going to correct him in front of the girls. We leave and start driving home and when we get to the point where we can see the New York City skyline I remember we all just stared because it was really weird seeing it with towers gone.

KATE

I am concerned about Bob but I think he probably went downtown after the buildings collapse and I imagine him down there pulling people out of the rubble. There was no way for me to get home to New Jersey by train that day because the trains stopped. The only way I could get home was by boat. There were all kinds of boats picking people up on the west side of Manhattan and taking them across the Hudson River and so I walked to the west side and stood on a line with about 1000 other people waiting for a ride. I ended up on an Army Corp of Engineers boat and take it to New Jersey. I arrive and there are lots of people just staring over at Manhattan and watching in disbelief at the terrible scene across the river. I walk to a train station just in time to catch a train back to my parent's house. There is a conductor on the train but he isn't collecting tickets. Some people are soaking wet because if you were covered in dust you had to be literally hosed down to remove any contaminants before you got on the train. I get to my parents house about 8 o'clock that evening and my Dad picks me up at the train station and when my Dad sees me he gives me a big bear hug and just starts to cry. It is the first time in my life that I have seen him cry. He says "We have to pray, Katie, we have to pray for Bob."

DESIREE

Because I'm one of the last employees to leave my office I think that everyone else has gotten out as well. The next day I return home to New Jersey and one of my bosses calls and starts naming people asking if I had seen any of the following employees because they are missing. I think about Jim and how I saw him making sure that everyone was out of the office. Jim's name is one of the names on the list.

BRIDGET

My cousin's wife called the hospitals in the area and posts Joe's picture everywhere and anywhere she can. She hoped he was knocked out somewhere and had amnesia -- maybe someone had taken him in. I felt every emotion on that day -- fear, sorrow, denial. But the strongest emotion I felt was anger.

GERRY

After leaving the Trade Center I walked north to 35th Street to an office where I knew some people and could get to a phone to try and call my family. I finally got through to my sister at 11:30. I then continued to walk north to 96th Street where my daughter was at her school. After getting my daughter I met a neighbor of mine who was in Manhattan with his car. He drove us back to my home in the Bronx. When I finally stumbled through our back door it was 5PM. The next moment, my wife and I were holding each other.

RAY

My wife and I had just moved to a new apartment in Brooklyn. She was a great cook and ironically cooked her first pasta meal in the new place on September 10th. When she didn't come home (and she was a strong woman, she would have found a way) it changed my life dramatically. I had to submit DNA evidence and file for a death certificate, which I never imagined I would have to do. New York City gets a bad rap for being a cold-hearted city but it is not true. This city could not have been nicer to me and all the other families. We all were invited to come down to the site and when I did come down there were a lot of tourists around and I remember thinking this is not a tourist attraction. But you come to live with that just like Pearl Harbor. This is where everyone, when they come to New York City, they want to see it.

PAUL

When I think of the Trade Center that night, when I close my eyes and I remember what I saw it was papers; papers swirling, never stopping just swirling around and around. I don't see one piece of furniture or anything to show that this used to be office space. No water coolers or desks or chairs no keyboards or anything like that. We were sure that there were still people alive in the debris and we start to search. There's been lots of building collapses and not everybody dies. Around midnight they take a cop out and then in the morning they take a few more people out and that's it. Nobody else is taken out of the rubble alive.

GAIL

We go to a friend's apartment and in an odd coincidence some of our neighbors are also staying in that same building so right away a loose coalition of people from our building forms. Some of them were at work that morning so they are asking us if the building is even still there. After two weeks we get word that we will be allowed a 15-minute police escorted visit back into our apartment. We go back for that 15 minute visit there is a huge perimeter fence up around the area. When they swing that fence open and we walk down my street I just start to weep. Everything looked bombed and burned and blasted. The High School where I had been voting has "morgue" spray painted on the side. They are using the cafeteria freezers and refrigerators as temporary morgue space.

ANTHONY

I decided that I would volunteer to come down here. I was not assigned to come down here I volunteered. Where I live in New Jersey, I am also a volunteer firefighter. When 9/11 happened I said to myself I know what the New York City firefighters are going to go through. I will never, make no mistake, compare myself to a New York City firefighter because they are the elite of the elite. But I thought I have a job where I'll be able to help the firefighters. I could move a piece of steel for them and maybe make their job easier so they can find survivors so that was my motivation for volunteering to work the site.

BOB

They took me to the hospital because I had a fractured skull and nerve trauma to my neck. Both my shoulders are fractured, I had a broken nose and 6 fractured toes. My hearing also went. I have no idea how I got any of those injuries.

ANN

The fire department came to my house late that night. My

daughters had gone to bed in my bed and about midnight I heard two car doors close and a knock on my door. It was Charlie, Bruce's lieutenant and another firefighter. They kind of hemmed and hawed for a few seconds and finally I said "just say it". And Charlie said they are unaccounted for. I asked how many from Squad 41 and they said Bruce plus 5 others. I asked who they were. It was everyone on duty. The entire crew was unaccounted for.

GERRY

The attacks on the World Trade Center were considered to be two 5-alarm fire events. 5 alarm was the highest response in New York City at the time and 2000 firefighters responded to the site along with a similar number of police officers. 343 firefighters, 37 Port Authority Police and 23 New York City Police officers and several emergency medical technicians were killed. It is estimated that there were about 1,400 people at or above the crash zone in the north tower and 600 at or above the crash zone in the south tower. And these people were either trapped and died in the collapses or they were killed in the initial plane crashes. When you add up those 400 uniformed victims with those trapped or killed by the crashes you realize that less than 400 people died everywhere else in the complex. That means that if you had an option to get out you probably did. 2,753 people were killed at the World Trade Center on 9/11. 2,977 people including the Pentagon and Shanksville, PA.

KATE

That night I called Bob's firehouse and there is still no information so they took my number and said that someone would call me back. I try to go to sleep but I can't so I turn on the TV and I see the end of a press conference with Mayor Giuliani and Commissioner Von Essen of the fire department. It was a little after 11pm when they announced that over 300 firefighters were missing. And when I hear that number, that's when I know that Bob is probably gone and everything has just changed forever.

LIGHTS / SOUND - a short pause.

PART IV: RECOVERY

BRIDGET

My friend Rita's father suggested that instead of going around being angry I should use that energy and volunteer for the Salvation Army. I go in for an interview and they ask me what talent I have. Talent? I have no talent. I can't think of anything. Finally I say 'Well, I'm Italian.' They look at me. I say, "I'm Italian, I can cook!" So they assign me to the food truck at the Medical Examiners Office. I work one 12-hour shift every Thursday. The Salvation Army food truck is on the sidewalk on 31st Street and facing it are the refrigerated trucks where the remains of the victims are stored. We have a 4 burner stove run on a generator, a grill, an icebox. We have no running water, no heat, and no air conditioning. We have to use a hose in street to wash our hands and utensils. There are no bathrooms – an apartment building 3 blocks away offers us theirs. We make our menus based on what is donated that day. I run around trying to make the best grilled cheese sandwiches, the best tuna melts, the best cup of coffee. My 84-year old mother sends me in with a cake she makes every week and I put a sign on it "Grandma Lu's homemade pound cake". It's gone in 10 minutes.

KATE

All around the city, everywhere you look, is the American flag. Big flags, small flags are everywhere. I don't go back to work and within a few days I get a packet of letters from the people I work with. That was the first kind of support I got and it just continued from there. Letters from people around the country and the world and statues from different fire departments and quilts and teddy bears and drawings were sent to me and it was just overwhelming. Packages were simply addressed "To the family of firefighter Bob McPadden, Engine 23, FDNY" and they would get to me. The loss was so deep and personal but because of that mail I felt that everyone all over the world was reaching out to me and trying to comfort me.

BOB

It took me 5 months to go back. When I did go back it was too much for me and I had to go to therapy. Within 6 months time I did have a heart attack and that ended my career as a fire fighter.

PAUL

I was put out of the fire department on a lung disorder and I knew I couldn't go back to the site. The union put out word that at some of the firefighters funerals there were just a few people from the fire department in attendance and they could not have that. So I put on my uniform and started going to funerals because it's a tradition in the fire department that if there is a line of duty death you go to the funeral and stand outside. Sometimes there would be three funerals in one day.

ANN

A few days later I came to the site with my girls via in a FDNY van. When we got to the George Washington Bridge and there were men standing there in full military uniforms with the biggest guns I had ever seen in my life and my first thought was "This is the United States of America …we don't have military on bridges" And then when I looked at the skyline I couldn't place where the Towers had been and my sister said to me you thought there was going to be a cut out or something. I went to the site on the 28th of September with the fire department by boat from the Brooklyn Naval Yard. They picked me up in one of those fire department vans and it took forever to get into the city because the same thing… all the guys with the guns stopping everyone… and then we got on a boat in Brooklyn and went with the Red Cross over to North Cove marina in Battery Park City. The Red Cross gave my two girls teddy bears before we got off the boat. And then we walked underneath the walkway and stood on the corner of Liberty and West Street. I was in a group of 25 people and as we walked in the National Guard took their hats off and that to me was like "wow, this is real." The site looked like war to me, like you were in a bad war movie. And the smell and the sound…it was so loud. There was a pregnant woman with us and they gave her a mask to put on which in retrospect I think we all should have had on. And they gave me a hand drawn map that showed where you were standing and where the different buildings would have been. And the other sound I remember, besides the sound of the heavy equipment, was at one point my daughter Meghan suddenly just got hysterical.

Looking at the site was the reality. You could tell that there was nobody in there.

KATE

It was so difficult because Bob just disappeared. I talked to him that morning at 8:15 and he was so happy and excited about our move and then he was just gone. I decided to have a memorial service on September 29th. There were a dozen other fire fighters services that same day but despite this about three thousand people came including several hundred fire fighters. I used a helmet in place of the casket. In March of 2002 I got a phone call that Bob's remains have been identified through DNA. I decided to do just an immediate family only burial. About a year and a half later I'm talking to one of my widow friends and she told me that she called up the medical examiners office and they said they had found more remains of her husband. At that point I think that maybe I should be more pro active and so I call the office and sure enough they have found additional remains. So I had them collected and buried. After that I refilled out the family form and said I'm done. I checked 'don't notify me any more' if more remains were found.

GAIL

Pier 94, a passenger ferry terminal in Manhattan, was set up for anyone who was affected. Family members are told to go there to file missing persons reports, submit DNA samples, apply for death certificates, and meet with people from the Red Cross and the Salvation Army. After 9/11 I had to get my first cell phone because I had no home. I made so many calls that my first bill is over $600. I had no money coming in and no home to work from so I freak out and go to Pier 94 for help.

The Red Cross tells me about an organization on the pier called Safe Horizons. They ask me if I have a business certificate. I say yes and they say "give us that bill and we will pay it for you." Safe Horizons collected donations from people all across the country and helped a lot of people who were displaced to pay their bills.

RAY

36 thousand units of blood were donated on September 11th from people all over the tristate area but only 258 were used. There were less than 200 intact bodies found on the site but over 20 thousand body parts were recovered. However, more than 1100 people have never been identified and over 40 percent of the families involved got nothing back.

ANTHONY

The debris pile was close to 7 stories high and right away thousands of people from all over the world volunteered to help out with the recovery. You had fire fighters and police officers but you also had construction workers and ironworkers and you needed people like that to work the heavy equipment. I drove a truck in the middle of the pile. Steel and debris from the WTC would be loaded onto my truck and I'd drive it out to a barge in the Hudson River. That debris would then be taken to Staten Island and there they had people sift through it looking for remains or any personal items that might help identify people that were missing. Another thing I did was to take a fire hose and hook it up to any fire hydrant that might be working and wash down all the buildings. All that smoke and dust had to be washed off. As soon as you washed down one building you'd turn around and there'd be dust all over another building so it was a non-stop operation. All the workers and the

500 thousand volunteers that came down here to help, all those people had to be fed and all that garbage had to be thrown out so I did that too. But I tell you with a humble heart that it was nothing compared with what other people had to do.

GERRY

By September 14th I was back at work trying to get new office space ready with a skeleton crew. A lot of people who work in the private sector were back at work the next day. We were relocated to Queens in emergency space but there wasn't enough room for everyone. My desk was in a utility room for several months. The first time we all got together as a staff was in a conference room in midtown the Monday after the attacks. It was really intense. I don't know if I can put into words exactly how it felt, it was just a really intense experience.

DESIREE

My company was back up and running again on September 13th but I didn't go back to work until the following Monday. We had an office in midtown and were relocated there. They had counselors on hand which was a good thing because that first day back day was basically a crying fest. I actually needed to go back to work because I needed to see other survivors from my office. There was a lot of hugging and a lot of tears. We all went into a conference room and shared stories. It was really important for me to be with people who had gone through the same thing.

BRIDGET

They found a piece of Joe's elbow at the southwest corner of West Street. His wife, Marie, had a memorial service. All in all 8 pieces of my cousin were found and identified within the first year after the attacks. She says there is no resolve.

ANTHONY

One day a fire chief asked me to come with him to the morgue. I got a very eerie feeling when he asked me that, I don't know why. Next to the morgue you could smell chemicals and you could smell death. You remember those kinds of smells. I waited outside the morgue for the fire chief and after a few minutes he came out and handed me a bunker coat and pants, a scott pack and a mask and he asked me to please throw them away. That was the most difficult thing I had to do in my life because I didn't think a firefighters uniform belonged in a garbage truck. That was early on. Thankfully, I wasn't asked to do that ever again.

KATE

What I found out happened to Bob took several months to piece together from several different accounts. Bob and the men of Engine 23 got there a little after 9am, which would have been just after the second plane, hit the South Tower. Engine 23 was assigned to go into the Marriott hotel and rescue any remaining hotel guests and employees. When the south tower collapsed it fell right on top of the Marriott hotel and split that building in two. And there were some people that survived that collapse but Bob and the four other men he was with from Engine 23 did not.

RAY

In January I was contacted by the police department and they asked me to come down to the medical examiners office.

They were able to positively identify Barbara's remains via DNA evidence. Now I know this was not going to be easy. My only hope was that she didn't suffer. With what I saw in that small box of her remains I knew that was the case. It was instantaneous ending for her, which is all I could have asked for. We were friendly with a group of nuns in Staten Island called the Daughters of Saint Paul and they helped me put together a nice memorial for Barbara. I had to give the eulogy, which was tough, but I did it and I felt better for it. Did it give me closure? No. You never close the door, you never forget.

ANN

March 2002 I got a telephone call in the middle of the night that they had found Bruce's body. He was in the South Tower. Only two bodies from Squad 41 were ever found. Bruce's death certificate came in the mail and the thing I remember most about the death certificate is that under "cause of death" it said homicide.

BOB

The recovery lasted 8 Months and 19 Days until May 30, 2002. The digging went down to bedrock and every piece of dust, steel and tissue has all been accounted for. Credit cards, keys, pagers, personal items and what not were all catalogued and returned to the families if possible. Most of the steel that they recovered at the site was recycled and 7 tons of that steel was made into the bow of a new Navy ship. The ship was christened in November of 2009 the USS New York. The motto of this ship is "Never Forget".

ANTHONY

I got to know some of the firefighters down at the site very well and if they needed anything from me all they had to do was ask and I would do it. I never told my boss because I didn't really care. I can say that now because I retired about 4 years ago. Every time a body was recovered at the site they would sound three alarms. When you heard those alarms everybody at the site would come to a complete stop. And I mean there was complete silence because everyone knew what was happening.

BRIDGET

Whenever we heard sirens we knew it meant that more remains had been found and are headed our way. We all instinctively stopped what we were doing and put our hands over our hearts as the ambulances passed on their way to the morgue. I tried not to cry and said a silent prayer to myself.

ANTHONY

If it was a civilian that they found, they would put that person in a stokes basket and put the body in an ambulance and take it to the medical examiners office up on 32nd street where they would try to identify the remains. They spent many years trying to identify all remains. The remains they could not identify are in the September 11th Memorial and Museum. But to this day, they are still identifying remains.

DESIREE

For the first year I often thought I was OK. If someone asked "how are you?" my reply was always the same, "fine". I was alive so I was fine. But a group of women survivors I work with created "Bathroom Therapy Sessions". We would meet in the women's room and check in with each other to see if we were all going through the same thing. Our emotions ranged from anger at the insensitivity of management who told us to "get back to normal" to survivor's guilt. Some in our group thought that if they had only run down the corridors of the floor and alerted everyone to evacuate more lives would have been saved. We had to reassure them that there was nothing wrong with our building, so technically there was no need to evacuate. No one ever suspected that a second plane was coming. It took me 14 months to feel a semblance of normal again.

PAUL

It took the fire department a year and three months to bury the dead. Many had more than one funeral because they had a memorial before they found any remains and then a funeral when they found remains. It was all very, very sad.

GERRY

The recovery from the attacks was one of the strangest times of my life. Every work day I would join my dazed colleagues in our emergency office space in Queens and try to make believe we were working toward a normalcy that could never be achieved. But each day we were harshly reminded that everything had changed. We helped to bury our 3 colleagues who had been killed – Ignatius Adanga, Charles Lesperance and See Wong Shum - as well as a huge part of our lives, or so it seemed. We were all post-traumatic to one extent or another and we labored to keep functioning under a bizarre cascade of new threats: real, rumored and imagined. Still we trudged in and tried to set things right. But the reality was never far away. Slowly, over time, something like normalcy did take hold. After three years, we moved back to lower Manhattan and that reopened a lot of scars. Time does heal, but it does not remove the wounds.

GAIL

We moved back into our apartment right before Christmas of 2002 so we were out 15 months. It can get depressing living right there and having those reminders every day. When that happens I think to myself there were 19 guys in those planes out to do their worst and they did bad. But afterwards 500 thousand people came down here to volunteer and more would have come if they could.

LIGHTS / SOUND - a short pause.

PART V: PERFORMING TRIBUTE

PAUL

I came down to the World Trade Center to look for survivors but I didn't find any. In the days that followed I found out that I had lost 46 of my friends. I lost true friends or my friends sons. People who I flipped burgers with and drank beer in the backyard with. I couldn't save my friends but I can tell the story of 9/11. If I couldn't save them I can try to save their memories.

GAIL

By January of 2002 I was on the ragged edge and so I joined a survivor's therapy group to try to get over it until I realized that I was never going to get over it. This is always going to be a part of me so talking about it is a part of accepting it. It's a way for me to speak before people like you who want to pay tribute and remember together. Its hard work remembering and I thank you for it.

GERRY

Around Thanksgiving I was in lower Manhattan to attend a meeting in a building near the World Trade Center site. On the way to the meeting I found myself standing in front of Saint Paul's Chapel, a small church right across the street from ground zero. The iron fence around Saint Paul's had been transformed into an impromptu memorial with signs and posters of the victims and mementos sent from around the world. Many people were milling about in front of the fence. On the sidewalk in front of the chapel was a rickety music stand on which a notebook had been placed for people to record their thoughts. After staring at the notebook for a bit I walked up to it and wrote "I got out of the World Trade Center on September 11th and I'm very sorry for those who did not." That is why I do volunteer work at the site and why I tell my story.

RAY

I am a part of 9/11. I didn't choose to be but I am. I don't want Barbara's memory to be forgotten. My wife was so quiet. She was a very private person if she knew that I was talking about her to people she didn't know she might not be pleased but I'll take that chance. The most private person I knew is now tied to the most public event in our nation's history. That's fate. It's a cliché, but you really do never know what's going to happen tomorrow so I try to appreciate, as best I can, what I have today.

KATE

I really thought late, late that night on September 11 that

my life was over. But I hold in my heart a story my grandmother told me. Her youngest brother fought over in Germany in WWII, and he had a young wife at home and they had no children. He used to write her letters and in one of the last letters he wrote her, before he was killed in the war, he said if something happens to me, don't let this war ruin two lives. They took 2,753 lives at the World Trade Center that day but they didn't take mine. And I think it's a credit to Bob and to all those who died to make the most of this life.

BOB

Telling my story is part of my therapy so I'll probably be telling it for the rest of my life. It helps me. I hope it never happens again. It can happen again. I don't know what the answer is to stop it. All of the men I brought into the city with me on that day survived. Two of them got banged up pretty badly. The third guy, who was the youngest, walked away from the whole thing and just got dirty. If I had to do it all over again I would gladly do it because it was my job.

DESIREE

This is my tribute to my co-workers, the 171 AON employees who were killed on September 11, 2001 and the ones who survived with me. It's my way of keeping the memories and the story of 9/11 alive.

ANTHONY

9/11 was the worst time in my entire life. But it was also the best time in my life because I got to meet some very wonderful people. And now I get to stand here and tell you my story and I want to tell you that you honor me by listening. Today you probably did more for me and everyone else here then we did for you because we need to talk about this to heal inside. And tonight you have allowed me to heal inside that much more. We must remember the people we lost but we must also remember all the good things that people did for others after 9/11 and keep doing them.

BRIDGET

I do this to never forget, to never become complacent. Volunteering with the Salvation Army forced me out of my comfort zone. I got a chance to look into the eyes of people from all over the world, people of different cultures, different races, different religions and I never once saw adversity. What I did see was what we have in common – a belief in each other. I am not angry any more because I've replaced my anger with hope.

ANN

I believe strongly in the concept of person to person history. Sharing my story is my way of connecting you to the real people of September 11th. When I talk about Bruce, he's more that just a number or just a statistic. I hope that for you Bruce is real. And everyone has to be real for it to matter.

GERRY

We are grateful for this opportunity to pay tribute to the people who died and the people who lived. When the Twin Towers were completed the architect, Minoro Yamasaki, said the World Trade Center will be a living symbol of man's dedication to world peace. Today on the site where his enormous towers once stood brand new buildings stand and a beautiful tree-lined memorial and museum is complete. We hope that you will share your stories and your strengths with one another. Thank you for listening to ours and for helping us all to remember.

LIGHTS FADE

THE END

Bios

Gerry Bogacz works for the New York Metropolitan Transportation Council and was on the 82nd floor of North Tower in both the 1993 and September 11th attacks.

Desiree Bouchat is a consultant with AON Corporation and is a survivor of the South Tower.

Bridget Damiano lost her cousin, Joseph Pick, in the South Tower on September 11th. She was also a volunteer with the Salvation Army from September 2001 until the end of the recovery in May 2002.

Gail Langsner is a resident of Lower Manhattan and lived on the 12th Floor of an apartment building on Liberty Street opposite the South Tower. On the morning of September 11th, she was out voting at her local high school when the first plane hit the North Tower. Gail was not able to return to her home for over fifteen months after the attacks.

Paul McFadden is a retired firefighter who worked in Rescue

2 in Brooklyn and was involved in the rescue and recovery effort after September 11th.

Bob Nussberger is a retired volunteer firefighter from Broad Channel, New York.

Kate Richardson lost her husband, firefighter Bob McPadden of Engine 23 on September 11th. Bob and Kate were in the process of moving to Pearl River, NY, days before September 11th and were married for 3 years. Kate has since remarried and has two young sons. She is a Professor of Management at Pace University.

Ann Van Hine Ann's husband, Bruce, was killed in the line of duty on September 11th. Bruce worked as a firefighter for Squad 41 in the Bronx. Ann is the author of the memoir "Pieces Falling."

Ray Habib Ray's wife, Barbara, was a Senior V.P at Marsh & McLennan for almost thirty years. Her primary office was in Midtown Manhattan but on September 11th she was attending a meeting at the Marsh & McLennan offices on the 99th floor of the North Tower.

Anthony Palmeri worked for the New York City Department of Sanitation for 23 years. After September 11th he volunteered to work the recovery at the site.

About the author

In October of 2005 Donna Kaz became a volunteer for the Tribute Center in New York City and began leading tours of the former site of the original World Trade Center. All Tribute Center docents have a connection to September 11 and share their stories during their tours. Kaz, who lost her cousin on 9/11 and lived in the area, was inspired by the many stories she heard and believed that weaving them into a theatre piece would allow more people to honor the memories of those lost and those who survived. "Performing Tribute 9/11" was developed in 2006 and first presented in 2007. The play now includes ten stories of resilience and courage among September 11 survivors, family members, first responders, area residents and recovery workers. For more information visit www.performingtribute.com

Donna Kaz is a multigenre writer and activist based in New York. www.donnakaz.com @donnakaz

Acknowledgments

Thanks to the Common Ground Community, The Tribute Center, The September 11 Memorial and Museum, Endurance Theatre, Sarah Locke, Ann Warren, Tracy Turner, Sonia Agron, Rita Weiner, Manhattan Community Arts Fund, The Port Authority of NY and NJ, Daniel Brodie, Dan Hansell, Fred Sager, Deb Di Grigorio, Shannon Curry Green, Richard Charkham.

PHOTOS

Bruce Van Hine (photo courtesy of Ann Van Hine)

Bridget Damiano with other Salvation Army
volunteers. (front row, third from left)

Bob McPadden (Photo courtesy of Kate
Richardson)

(L to R) Paul McFadden, Kate Richardson, Ann Van Hine, Gail Langsner, Bridget Damiano, Gerry Bogacz. Photo: Donna Kaz

(L to R) Desiree Bouchat, Anthony Palmeri, Ann Van Hine, Gail Langsner, Gerry Bogacz. Photo: Donna Kaz

(L to R) Bridget Damiano, Donna Kaz, Gerry Bogacz, Kate Richardson, Ann Van Hine, Gail Langsner, Paul McPadden. Photo: David W. Dunlap/The New York Times)

Patch created by Bob Nussberger and worn by the Broad Channel Volunteer Fire and Ambulance Corp. crew.

13"x11"

ENDURANCE
THEATRE
NY, NY
P-0009.001

At each presentation of the original cast of
Performing Tribute 9/11, a piece from the
cladding of the towers was displayed. The Port
Authority of New York and New Jersey distributed
pieces of the World Trade Center rubble to
organizations and cities around the world for
memorials. **Endurance Theatre** received a small
piece in August of 2010 to tour with the
production.

The 176 employees of AON lost on September
11th. Photo courtesy of Desiree Bouchat

Praise for "Performing Tribute 9/11"

"A profound performance that shows the heroism of people who have chosen to respond to devastation and hatred with quiet determination and a belief that they can and will make the world a better place." --

Michael Arad, Designer of the World Trade Center Memorial

"Ten stories of 9/11 told by family members, survivors, first responders, volunteer workers, and residents are woven together in this dramatic and groundbreaking theater piece."

Stefan Pryor, former President, Lower Manhattan Development Corporation